Dear Parents and Educators,

Welcome to Penguin Young Readers! As pa[rents] •
know that each child develops at his or her own
speech, critical thinking, and, of course, readin[g]
Readers recognizes this fact. As [a result, each]
book is assigned a traditional e[asy-to-read level]
Guided Reading Level (A–P). B[oth levels help you determine]
the right book for your child. Pl[ease see the back cover]
for specific leveling informatio[n. Penguin offers]
esteemed authors and illustrat[ors, beloved characters,]
fascinating nonfiction, and m[ore!]

Backyard Chickens

LEVEL **3**

GUIDED
READING
LEVEL **L**

This book is perfect for a **Transitional Reader** who:
• can read multisyllable and compound words;
• can read words with prefixes and suffixes;
• is able to identify story elements (beginning, middle, end, plot, setting, characters, problem, solution); and
• can understand different points of view.

Here are some **activities** you can do during and after reading this book:
• Nonfiction: Nonfiction books deal with facts and events that are real. Talk about the elements of nonfiction. Discuss some of the facts you learned about chickens. Then answer the following questions: Where can you raise chickens? Name three different breeds, or types, of chickens. What is a chicken home called? What food do chickens eat? At what age will hens start laying eggs?
• Make Connections: Many people raise chickens in their backyards. Discuss how you can become a backyard chicken farmer. What do you need to raise chickens?

Remember, sharing the love of reading with a child is the best gift you can give!

—Bonnie Bader, EdM
   Penguin Young Readers program

*Penguin Young Readers are leveled by independent reviewers applying the standards developed by Irene Fountas and Gay Su Pinnell in *Matching Books to Readers: Using Leveled Books in Guided Reading*, Heinemann, 1999.

For Anne, the Briggs family's first backyard-chicken owner—AR

PENGUIN YOUNG READERS
Published by the Penguin Group
Penguin Group (USA) LLC, 375 Hudson Street, New York, New York 10014, USA

USA | Canada | UK | Ireland | Australia | New Zealand | India | South Africa | China

penguin.com
A Penguin Random House Company

Photo credits: cover (from foreground to background): © Thinkstock/cynoclub, © Thinkstock/David De Lossy, © Thinkstock/Anatolii Tsekhmister, © Thinkstock/ChickiBam, © GettyImages/Horst Gerlach; flap: © Thinkstock/Jupiterimages; page 3: © Thinkstock/Diana Taliun; page 4: (chicken) © Thinkstock/Evgeniy1, (apple core) © Thinkstock/Mega_Pixel; page 6: (Manhattan Bridge) © Thinkstock/Samuel Borgesl, (chicken) © Thinkstock/Evgeniy1; page 7: © Thinkstock/leisuretime70; page 8: © Thinkstock/Lusoimages; page 9: © Thinkstock/ewastudio; pages 10–11: © Thinkstock/SherryL18; page 12: © Thinkstock/andrewburgess; page 13: (Easter Egger) © Getty Images/james knighten, (leghorn) © Thinkstock/Anne Connor; page 14: © Thinkstock/Toa55; page 15: © Thinkstock/GlobalP; page 17: © Thinkstock/Terry Wilson; pages 18–19: © Thinkstock/ErikaMitchell; page 20: © Thinkstock/Vrabelpeter1; page 21: © Thinkstock/Comstock Images; pages 22–23: © getty images/getty image; page 24: © Thinkstock/murengstockphoto; page 25: © getty images/Design Pics/Ron Nickel; page 26: © Thinkstock/Stephanie Frey; page 27: © Thinkstock/Arpad Nagy-Bagoly; page 28: © Thinkstock/rubisco67; page 29: © Thinkstock/RandallJSylvia; page 30: © Thinkstock/IvonneW; page 31: © Thinkstock/hotshotanne; page 32: © Thinkstock/Songquan Denge; page 33: © Thinkstock/jurgenfr; pages 34–35: © Thinkstock/Wavebreakmedia Ltd; page 36: © Thinkstock/Adam88xx; page 37: © Thinkstock/Image Source Pink; page 38: © Thinkstock/Wavebreakmedia Ltd; page 39: © Thinkstock/murengstockphoto; page 40: © Thinkstock/hotshotanne; page 41: © Thinkstock/greenleaf123; page 42: © Thinkstock/Digital Vision; page 43: (toast) © Thinkstock/nito100, (plate) © Thinkstock/Miriam2009; page 44: © Thinkstock/wathanyu0; page 45: © Thinkstock/anna1311; page 46: © Thinkstock/Arpad Nagy-Bagoly; page 47: © Thinkstock/Arpad Ariusz Nawrocki; page 48 © Thinkstock/Jupiterimages.

Text copyright © 2015 by Avery Reed. All rights reserved. Published by Penguin Young Readers, an imprint of Penguin Group (USA) LLC, 345 Hudson Street, New York, New York 10014. Manufactured in China.

ISBN 978-0-448-48720-5 (pbk)   10 9 8 7 6 5 4 3 2 1
ISBN 978-0-448-48721-2 (hc)   10 9 8 7 6 5 4 3 2 1

Backyard Chickens

by Avery Reed

Penguin Young Readers
An Imprint of Penguin Group (USA) LLC

Peck, peck, peck!

This chicken is eating a treat. She is free to run and play all day.

At night, she sleeps in a safe home. Does she live on a farm?

No! She lives in a backyard in New York City.

Today, you do not have to live on a farm to have chickens. You can have chickens right in your own backyard.

Let's find out how you can raise chickens, too!

A female chicken is called a hen.

A male chicken is called a rooster (say: ROO-ster).

Before you get a hen or a rooster, have a grown-up check the laws in your town or city.

There are rules about how many chickens you can own and where you can keep them.

Many places will not let you have a rooster, because they are very noisy.

Cock-a-doodle-doo! Roosters crow when the sun comes up.

Pick out which breed, or kind, of chicken you want to raise. There are many different chicken breeds.

Rhode Island Reds (say: rohd EYE-land) live well in a backyard.

RHODE ISLAND RED

Easter Eggers (say: EE-ster EG-er) are good for backyards, too, because they are quiet.

Leghorn (say: LEG-horn) chickens lay lots of eggs.

> EASTER EGGER <

> LEGHORN <

You can buy chickens from a store called a hatchery (say: HATCH-er-ee).

A hatchery may be far from where you live. That's okay. The hatchery will send you chickens in the mail!

You can buy eggs to hatch. Or you can buy chicks that are one day old. You can also buy older chickens that are ready to lay eggs.

Look! These chicks came today.

They are one day old.

Hold them gently in your hands.

Place the chicks in a brooder (say: BROO-der). This is where they will live for four to six weeks.

When they are young, the chicks will eat special food called starter feed. You can find starter feed at a local pet store or online.

Set their food in a bowl on one end of the brooder.

On the other end, place fresh water.

The chicks will run back and forth. They will grow up strong and healthy.

Chicks need to be warm. Put a
heat lamp in the brooder.
If they are cold, the chicks will
group together.

If they are hot, they will stand by the wall.

If they are happy, they will say, "Cheep! Cheep!"

Play with your chicks.

Hold them.

Talk to them.

You can even sing to them!

Each chick is different. Some will like to run. Others will want to sit in your lap. Some will chirp a lot.

Others will be very quiet.

But all chicks will eat from your hand!

Soon, the chicks grow feathers.
They are ready to live outside.
Take them to their new home.
Their new home is called a coop
(say: KOOP).

A coop is a little house with a fence around it. The fence makes an area called the run. The run is a place where the chickens can eat and play.

Inside the little house, there is a bar across the top. The bar is called a roost. The chickens will sleep standing on the roost.

There are also boxes in the house.
The hens will lay eggs in the boxes.

It is important to make sure your chickens are safe. Dogs, cats, hawks, raccoons, and other animals will want to eat the chickens. They will try to break into the coop.

To keep these animals out, the coop's fence needs to be very strong. Make sure the fence does not have any holes. And do not leave the fence door open at night.

When you are with your chickens, you can open the fence door. Your chickens will run all around your backyard.

They will eat lots of bugs and
worms. Yum! But do not forget to
close the door when playtime is over.

Adult chickens eat food called scratch. It is made of wheat and corn.

They also eat grit. Grit is made of small stones and sand.

You can buy chicken scratch and grit at a pet store or online.

Chickens love to eat strawberries, apples, bread, meat, and even eggshells.

Give your chickens fresh food and water every day. Clean the coop once a week. Good food, a clean home, and exercise will keep your chickens healthy.

But sometimes they will get sick. If your chickens do not feel better soon, take them to the animal doctor.

When they are six months old,
the hens will lay eggs. Most hens
lay one or two eggs every other day.
In the winter, hens lay fewer eggs.
Some hens lay white eggs. Others lay
brown eggs. Some lay green eggs!

Every morning, you can collect the eggs.

And you can eat them for breakfast.

Hens will lay eggs even if you do not own a rooster.

But hens can only have chicks with a rooster's help.

Look! This hen is ready to have chicks. In one week, she has laid eight eggs. Her group of eggs is called a clutch. She will sit on her clutch for 21 days.

Crack, crack, crack!

A chick is pecking a hole in its egg.

Soon, all the chicks have hatched.
You have eight new chicks to care for.

Now you are a backyard-chicken farmer!